The Overnight Children's Book Author

DR. SCHARMAINE LAWSON, NP

The Overnight Children's Book Author
Published by A DrNurse Publishing House New Orleans, Louisiana

Copyright @ 2023 Scharmaine Lawson, DNP, FNP, PMHNP, FAANP, FAAN
All rights reserved.
No part of this book may be reproduced or transmitted in any form or by
any means, electronic or mechanical, including photocopying, recording,
or by any information storage and retrieval system without the written
permission of the publisher, except where permitted by law.

A DrNURSE
PUBLISHING HOUSE
Published by
A DrNurse Publishing House
7041 Canal Blvd., New Orleans, La. 70124
www.DrLawsonNP.com

ISBN:
Paperback: 978-1-945088-47-6
ePub: 978-1-945088-50-6

Library of Congress Control Number: 2023901990
This book is printed on acid-free paper.
Printed in the United States of America

Dedication

Dear Skylar Rose, and Wyatt Shane, your ability to love me in spite of my many moods while writing continues to keep me suspended in awe and total adoration of you.

Dear Grandma, I miss you more than life. Thank you for the memories and your abiding spirit, which lives in me. You would be proud of the woman I've become because of your love, rearing, and nurturing. You adopted me at four-months old when you were at the tender age of 60 and somehow always "knew" that I would make something out of myself. I'm so glad you believed in me.

Income Disclaimer

This book contains business strategies, marketing methods and other business advice that, regardless of my own results and experience, may not produce the same results (or any results) for you. I make absolutely no guarantee, expressed or implied, that by following the advice below you will make any money or improve current profits, as there are several factors and variables that come into play regarding any given business.

Primarily, results will depend on the nature of the product or business model, the conditions of the marketplace, the experience of the individual, and situations and elements that are beyond your control.

As with any business endeavor, you assume all risk related to investment and money based on your own discretion and at your own potential expense.

Liability Disclaimer

By reading this book, you assume all risks associated with using the advice given below, with a full understanding that you, solely, are responsible for anything that may occur as a result of putting this information into action in any way, and regardless of your interpretation of the advice.

You further agree that our company cannot be held responsible in any way for the success or failure of your business as a result of the information presented in this book. It is your responsibility to conduct your own due diligence regarding the safe and successful operation of your business if you intend to apply any of our information in any way to your business operations.

Terms of Use

You are given a non-transferable, "personal use" license to this book. You cannot distribute it or share it with other individuals.

Also, there are no resale rights or private label rights granted when purchasing this book. In other words, it's for your own personal use only.

Foreword

Becoming a children's author is an industry that many would like to be a part of. Writing a book for the first time can seem daunting, especially if you have no experience or training, but it doesn't have to be this way. You do not need to take classes and return to school to become a successful writer in this industry. Many people would like to make money in the children's book market with little training. That is why this guide was written. It outlines all the steps you need to take to become a successful author in just 24 hours, which could start your journey toward being an established author. This book is meant to help new and experienced authors write, publish, and market their books.

The overnight children's book author addresses topics such as the importance of children›s books, how to write a children›s book, what exactly makes a good children›s book, bleed and formatting, book publishing and marketing, publishing companies, and many more. It gives you all the information you need to become a children's book author in just one day, which is excellent for busy people who don't know where to start. If you want to learn how to become a children's book author in just one day, I urge you to read this book and follow the outlined steps.

Table of Contents

Introduction................................ 13

CHAPTER ONE

The Importance of Children's Books 15

    What it is like to be
a children's writer................ 17

    The various genres
of children's books............... 19

CHAPTER TWO

How To Write A Children's Book 22

    Brainstorming story ideas 23

    Create interesting characters 25

    Plan your story 27

    Illustrations are important 29

    Interior children's books design 31

    Let your creativity flow............. 33

    Rhyming stories 36

CHAPTER THREE

What Exactly Makes A Good Children's Book? ...39

Bring pleasure to children during reading. ...42
Using a writing service to create a children's book ...44
Hiring freelance writers on Fiverr ...46
Writers from Upwork ...48
Content Writers forums ...51
Freelancers ...52
Children's Books Covers and Titles ...54
Titles and Subtitles ...56
Cover design rules ...58

CHAPTER 4

Book Bleed and Formatting ...63

What is a book bleed? ...63
What should you know about the book dimensions? ...65
The best bleed size for children's book. ...65
eBook formatting and its essence ...66

CHAPTER 5

Before Book Publishing and Marketing 69

Book Marketing 71
Copyright and Trademarks 73
Why should you care about
   copyright and trademarks? 74
Amazon book market research
   and tips. 75
Other marketing channels. 78
Marketing through Google Play 81
How to promote a children's book
   on Google Play 82
Ingram Spark 83

CHAPTER 6

Book Publishing 86

Traditional Publishing 86
Simple steps to publish children's
   books traditionally. 87
Self-publishing and its promise
   of freedom 89
Joint publishing 90
Vanity Publishing 92

CHAPTER 7

Book Publishing Companies............94

Trade Book Publisher............... 95
Book Packagers and Book
    Developers..................... 95
Book Packagers 96
Book Development Companies 97
"Bargain" Book Publishers 97
Textbook Publishers and
    Academic Publishers............ 98
Professional Publishers 99
Self-Publishing Services............ 101
Hybrid Publisher.................. 102

CHAPTER 8

ISBN and Different Prefixes 105

What children's book authors
    should know about ISBN 107

Conclusion........................... 109

Introduction

Yawl, I'm gonna keep this short and sweet. I wrote this book because soooooooooooo many folks have asked me for quick tips on how to write a children's book. With the tremendous success of Nola The Nurse®, many had a ton of questions.

Ergo, I wrote this book for all of you. It's meant to be simple, but effective to get you on your journey of children's book writing. You won't know it all, but every brand or dream starts with belief. Start there and never stop. We are so excited for your journey and will be cheering you on every step of the way.

Go Believe.
Go Dream.
Go Write.
Just Go.
Go
Go
Go

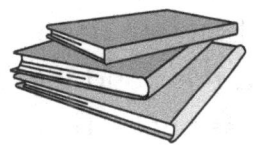

CHAPTER ONE

The Importance of Children's Books

Children's books are an integral part of their life. They learn many things from books and play with them, share their views about specific characters in the story, and become a part of it. Many experts believe that good children's books should be a prime source of building a child's personality. Good stories teach kids about different people, cultures, traditions, and values. In contrast, bad books will make them unable to differentiate between various norms and value systems. Every author and publisher should consider the quality of children's books to make good reading material for kids.

Fiction books are the simplest way to reach an understanding between people. Children learn and understand the world through stories and characters in these books. They read about other cultures, traditions, and lifestyles, which helps them form opinions. If we talk about bad fiction books written primarily for entertainment, they create stereotypes that distort their perception ability, while good ones bring out the various aspects of life closer to them, helping them understand its importance. These books provide insight into different characters and teach readers different values and cultural lessons.

Authors and publishers should consider specific points before writing a book for children. A good, educational children's book must have attractive illustrations which provide an idea about its character's children. It should also be written so that the story flows smoothly and leaves something good in their minds after reading it. The language used in children's books should be easy to understand and learn from.

What it is like to be a children's writer

Writing children's books is *not* the most straightforward job you can think of. If it were like that, everyone would do it. But this is one of the most challenging jobs because to make a story for kids targeted at specific age groups, you need to have an eye for details and paint pictures with words.

If you want to become a writer who writes stories for little kids between 3-10 years old, you will probably find writing a hard nut to crack if your writing has been chiefly adult-oriented thus far or if you've been writing stories targeted at adults. Kids have different tastes. Therefore, the writing should be geared towards a kid audience. A story that you used to find highly captivating, and fascinating might be something that a kid will brush off as if it's nothing.

That is why people who write children's books spend years trying to master the art. Their job is more than simply creating interesting characters and then putting them into exciting situations; it is more than just telling a story in a way to keep kids on their toes as they turn page after page of the book, eagerly waiting for what happens next. It's also ensuring your stories give an important message about life or other lessons so that the lectures remain with the little ones even when they have long outgrown the cute stories.

Having said that, if you are passionate about writing children's books and think you have what it takes to do this for a living, then ask yourself the following soul-searching questions:

- Why should I choose this topic?
- What are your strengths as a children's writer?
- What weaknesses do you wish to improve on?

Answer genuinely and work on your perceived weakness by learning how experts have done in the past. Yes, writing children's stories takes time and effort to master. But if you want it enough, you will make it happen one day. For now, get to know the different genres of children's books and how they are written.

The various genres of children's books

Different genres of children's literature are written in different styles. The genres are divided into two major categories, expository and fiction.

A particular type of fiction book is called a picture book. This genre has increased since its conception because young children like to look at colorful pictures while reading with adults. A picture book typically contains a single plot, is set in the present time, and takes place in one location. However, many picture books have been created over the past few decades.

Another type of fiction genre is chapter books. These novels contain more words than a picture book does. More words mean longer stories, and most chapters involve separate plots, each being resolved by the end of each chapter. A distinction between chapter books and novels for adults is that chapter books usually have about half a dozen to a dozen chapters, contributing to their shorter length than other forms of literature like novels for teenagers or young adults.

The expository genre is the easiest to distinguish because it features nonfiction books.

These books are based on facts and can be used by teachers, parents, or librarians when helping children learn new things—many nonfiction books, including science textbooks, historical works, biographies, and reference materials.

Another form of literature is the letter book, which contains stories about children who wrote letters to famous people and received a reply. These books enable young readers to see themselves in the protagonist's role and develop good communication skills through reading.

The last type of book is a chapter or picture storybook where both forms of literature coexist within one book. Picture storybooks contain illustrations and texts together on each page. Frequently, this genre features two separate plots; however, these can be intertwined if the author desires. One plot involves characters from fairy tales like the tooth fairy or the gingerbread man, while another deals with real-life issues such as moving out of their hometown or family members getting sick. The overall purpose of picture storybooks is to teach young children about real and fictional people and their situations in life.

An author should consider these factors when deciding which type of book to write: age, vocabulary level, setting, characters, and genre. The author can determine the best approach for writing their book with this information. Authors can choose from various genres to cater to a specific audience or satisfy consumer preferences in the children's literature market.

CHAPTER TWO

How To Write A Children's Book

As it turns out, writing a children's book is not much different from writing for adults. The process is the same: you have an idea for a story and then write, edit, revise, and re-edit until—voila! —it's ready to share with the world. But there's more than meets the eye behind writing great books for kids. So, what makes a children's book great? It all comes down to three things: solid content that appeals to young readers' imaginations, an engaging storyline their hearts will buy into, and relatable characters they'll want to root for.

One thing that sets children's books apart from other genres is their illustrations. A story can speak wonders all on its own, but it becomes a winning combination when paired with an engaging illustration. The most successful books are the ones that blend good storytelling with excellent illustrations to captivate young minds.

When plotting out your story, ask yourself questions like: What do I want to say? Is there something kids need to learn? Or perhaps you'd like to explore an exciting theme—friendship, freedom, teamwork, kindness—and build your story around it. Then think of your target age group and decide whether you'll write in prose or verse (or both) and whether there will be dialogue. A good rule of thumb is to keep your language simple, clear, and brief. And remember: When it comes down to making a story fun and exciting—go wild. Bring all your imagination into play and develop new ideas that captivate young readers' imaginations.

Brainstorming story ideas

Children's books such as the Harry Potter series and the Hunger Games trilogy appealed to readers with creative plots and relatable storylines.

One way to brainstorm creative storylines is by asking yourself these questions: What would I do if I had superpowers? What would happen if this happened instead of that? What happens when? Who does this character remind me of in real life, and why? How might things have changed if something else was different? How can my characters be involved in solving a mystery or standing up for something they believe in, like bullying at school or animal abuse?

Have trouble coming up with an idea for your book? You can also try writing down what you'd like to teach young children or what you want them to learn from your story. Once you've come up with several storylines, choose one that's the most interesting and has an overall positive message. And don't forget to make it simple and relatable. Children love stories about animals, toys coming alive at night, magic powers, and superheroes fighting evil. To make your children's story stand out, add a unique twist or a relatable character to the plot.

When you're done brainstorming storylines and working on developing your characters, it's time to get writing! Remember that this book is for young children who don't know how to read yet, so keep the vocabulary simple and short sentences. You can also have other adults or older siblings help you edit and proofread your story before submitting it to publishing companies.

> My Story: I was looking for children's books that discussed Advanced Practice Nurses and had melanin in their characters. These books did not exist. Sometimes you need to start with what doesn't exist to create what you would like to see exist. This fills a void in children's literature.

Create interesting characters

You must make the main character come alive. Now, this might sound like a strange thing to say, but it's essential.

If you give the child (or adult) reading your book a good understanding of who they are and what is going on with them, the whole story will seem much more accurate and exciting.

When writing a book, it's important to remember that children are reading the story.

To impact the reader, your villains should not be completely evil. An evil character saddens the child because he/she does not understand what is going on or why that person is acting that way. Instead of making these people appear bad in every way, try showing some good side, so the child feels sorry for this character rather than hate them.

To make someone seem interesting, show their feelings and respond to what other characters say or do. For example: If Violet was mean about her sister's hair, how would she react? She could be embarrassed or try to justify herself. It shows that she is interesting because you can see her good side coming out.

Another way to make characters more interesting is by explaining their motivations, what they want, and why. This method works very well with villains because the reader sees why someone has done something wrong and might relate to them somehow.

Also, give your character flaws to seem more natural to the readers. Make them act like human beings rather than flawless superheroes who always know what's happening around them without any problems.

Plan your story

The beginning is the most crucial part of writing a good children's book. It serves as an introduction to your story and hooks the reader's attention, especially younger ones. You want to create a curiosity that will make them continue reading until they reach the end of your book. As well as building suspense, you must remember that what you write must be simple enough for children to understand. The structure should closely follow how young kids think or talk about their actions or surroundings, usually simple sentences describing only one idea at a time- not always complete sentences depending on age group. They can describe things briefly but often leave out details immediately coming to mind.

For this reason, you need to make your story simple and full of action. Once they finish reading your book, they will be satisfied that they do not need any more information than what is provided in the text. There should be no extra explanations or vocabulary required to look up elsewhere. Everything must be included within the story to remain cohesive and simple yet interesting enough for children to understand and enjoy.

A good story beginning can look thus:

It was late in the night, and everything was quiet except for one little boy who could not sleep—he wanted to play! Poor little chubby bear didn't know that it was very late, and his mother was a light sleeper, and any little noise disturbed her rest. The cubby bear decided to visit his friend, the bunny rabbit, to play with him.

He sneaked out of bed and quietly walked across the room. He opened the door and tip-toed down the stairs – one step at a time, as he didn't want to wake anybody up. With such care, he let no one know that he was awake or had left home. Soon though, something happened that woke up some people.

A promising story flow can be seen in the example above, particularly for children.

Illustrations are important

A good illustration can enhance a child's enjoyment of their literature. Several people believe that if their children's books are exciting enough, they do not need illustrations. This is not the case since even adult readers who read full texts can get a lot from accompanying illustrations. Children's books can build different sentence structures and improve vocabulary.

You can also use children's books without illustrations to familiarize kids with print, practice reading aloud, and encourage them to read independently. If the texts are concise and include only a few sentences, your child can fill in some gaps using his imagination.

Illustrations help little children learn new words and provide visual information that enhances comprehension. As they do not understand everything they read or hear at first glance, illustrations enable them to take more from the text than written words. The benefit of illustrating literature for young readers is that they can see what characters look like and establish mental images of the story based on their own experiences. In this way, illustrations add depth and clarity to stories.

When choosing illustrations for your children's book, remember some things:

- You should ensure the pictures pull readers' eyes back to the text.
- Choose an exciting setting, pick colorful images,
- and do not forget about putting labels on them so that the reader (child) can talk about what he is looking at.

In addition, you may find it hard to illustrate your children's books yourself, many talented illustrators will help you create drawings for your kids' stories. Illustrations can improve children's understanding of literature and help them summarize texts. They provide visual information that enhances comprehension. So, it is important to choose interesting images. Each illustration should explain the written text.

Interior children's books design

Since the late 19th century, when children's books began being produced in mass quantities, their interior design has been a topic of interest to publishers and authors. Because children have different tastes from adults, an author must consider several things before deciding on a layout for his or her book. Will they prefer simplicity or color? Should pictures be included?

These questions are essential when designing the interior look of a children's book because children have less discretion than adults. Interior design used by publisher imprints can also influence a reader's impression of a book if it is aesthetically pleasing in some way. A well-designed interior can draw attention to a picture that might otherwise go unnoticed, making words more interesting and set the story's mood.

As for adults, design is usually second to format because they can appreciate both. For example, the choice between large or small font is not important to an adult reader unless it makes comprehension difficult. However, it can make a world of difference to a younger kid who has not yet mastered the basics of reading. This holds especially if children have trouble reading words too close together or have letters that don't stand out enough from the page.

A well-designed interior also establishes the mood of a story for young readers by including atmospheric images and text set off by interesting typography. While an author may want his work to be enjoyed by as many people as possible, the publisher's imprint will be determined by its appeal to children. Because what is aesthetically pleasing to adults and what appeals to children are often different, a publisher chooses which interior design elements will attract the attention of potential readers. A book's design may determine how much attention children give to the words.

Choosing an interior design for a child's book can influence what kind of story might attract their interest. A simple, to-the-point look for books for young readers might be more compelling than text that is self-consciously artistic because it makes reading interesting and unpretentious.

How words are set on the page can also affect how they are read by making characters seem larger or smaller than life. Even if a word is italicized or printed in a different color than the rest of the text, putting it above or below the rest makes it stand out immediately. A child can also absorb words on an illustrated background more easily than words set against a blank page, giving the impression of the pictures coming to life.

Interiors for children's books can use any number of colors and variations in font sizes and types. They aim to make reading easy and interesting, not attract attention through artistic design. Because illustrations are an integral part of almost every book intended for young readers, they should stand out from the text rather than get lost. This goal can be achieved by making images large enough to define them without clearly overwhelming them.

Let your creativity flow

When children's book authors write, they let their creative minds flow. However, this does not mean that they do not edit the story on the go or ignore grammar and punctuation rules. They simply allow themselves to enjoy writing by being open to new ideas. Even if some ideas are wonderful but are beyond the scope of what children can understand at a given age, authors feel free to put them aside. Authors often have an idea bank where fragmented scenes are kept long after the manuscript is completed. These scenes will then be used in upcoming projects. Authors must let their creative minds flow while writing children's books. If they hold back, it alters creativity and hampers their ability to find good ideas.

Inspiration can come from everyday experiences, the author's childhood, and real people. It is essential not to hold back the creative mind of an author, yet it must not go beyond the understanding capacity of children. There are a lot of 'universal' experiences that adults and children have in common, but there are also events that only affect one age group or another.

This will determine which scenes should be included in the story. Although children have very active imaginations, they still require scenes with descriptions as opposed to scenes where characters simply contemplate (Dialogues between characters such as "Where do you think we are?"; "I don't know"; "What do you mean, you don't know?"; "I don't know"; "You said that already!" do not work well in children's books).

Children's book authors must also take into consideration the way kids speak. Children like to hear their names mentioned and want things spelled out thoroughly (for example, they want to be told exactly what happens next). They are very impatient listeners; they will look elsewhere if something does not interest them immediately. If an author goes too far beyond the edge of comprehension, the child may feel even more confused than if he/she had stuck with perfectly understandable words. A light-hearted tone should prevail because this enhances creativity and allows children to enjoy other storytelling elements, such as humor. Although children have a vast imagination, they still want to hear a familiar story with a few variations. Children's book authors need to know what kind of child they are writing for and adjust accordingly.

Writing children's books is not just for kids – it is also rewarding for the author. It is a deep and fulfilling experience that can be shared with present-day children and future generations.

....

Seeing a story come alive in one's mind is exhilarating.

In conclusion, writing children's books means letting your creativity flow while considering the age group you are writing for and ensuring your story will keep their attention. In addition to adhering to standard grammatical standards, it is necessary to consider the kind of child you are writing for and to go beyond them at times. Ultimately, it is a fulfilling experience that should be shared with present-day children and future generations.

Rhyming stories

Rhythm is used to divide and organize writing into a pattern. Children's books often use rhythm to generate excitement and tension for the reader. Rhyming words will help tell your story with a steady beat. Here are some tips on how to incorporate rhythm in your book:

- Read your children's book out loud to see if it flows well. Limericks do not flow as well as other types of rhyming verse, so brainstorm strong ideas that will not be lost when read aloud.

- Choose a topic you would like to write about but ensure that there is enough material for a short story or poem with an ending that counts from five to ten. This will allow readers to anticipate the end.

- The first line should include words that rhyme but not necessarily with each other. This will build up excitement for the reader to see what word comes next in verse.

- Use alliteration (words that start with the same sound) to make your writing more interesting; it also will help you remember which words go together easier when writing children's books.

- Be sure to use descriptive words that appeal to kids' senses of sight, hearing, taste, and touch so that they can better imagine the scene as they read along. Illustrations can also describe surroundings if you cannot write pictures into your story.

- When using sentences within your writing, try to use shorter sentences that have a few descriptive words and action verbs (words like ran, jumped, and flew) instead of long sentences with several clauses (time modifiers such as before and after) because most children's books are read at an elementary level.

Once you've written the first draft of your children's book, review it for any missing words or awkward phrases and work on making edits until there are no more things to change.

Choose how many words will be in each line (this is called stanza form); this can depend on whether you want ten-syllable lines versus 12-syllable lines. Which determines the rhyme scheme; 5-7 syllables for each line are usually sufficient for children's books.

Once your children's book is complete, read it to a friend and family member and ask for their honest feedback, and go in and make edits based on their comments until you come up with a finished product with the help of professional editors.

CHAPTER THREE

What Exactly Makes A Good Children's Book?

In the world of children's literature, many titles come out in a year. There are many books to choose from and not enough time to read. But when a child hears about it or eventually gets their hands on it, they become obsessed with it. It becomes their favorite book, and they tell everyone who will listen. They want to read it repeatedly every night before bedtime. And if you're lucky, they might take pride in knowing how to read that book themselves! So, what exactly makes a good children's book?

For starters, these books should relate to their audience in one way or another. They must be able to hit home with them emotionally to feel connected through the story and the actual words written down. It needs to also capture interest from page one and keep building until it reaches its climax at the end, with a resolution for both characters and readers alike. Many components fit into this category, but when you get to it, these books become bestsellers because they hold onto certain essential pieces of what makes a good children's book.

The first and most crucial element is the message. Naturally, we want to ensure that we get children reading; however, their books need to be worth their time. They need to contain a strong theme that will stick with them for a long time. It can't just be something like "reading is fun," because then what's the point in publishing it? You would say things your readers already know or could figure out without buying a book about it!

The author needs to use characters and settings that children would find interesting and realistic in some way so they can relate and feel comfortable while following along with the story. We don't want kids thinking back on these stories years later and feeling confused about what happened or why they were so invested in the first place. Books must be able to give them an escape from reality without feeling distant or "not for them." It should feel familiar, almost like playing make-believe with their friends at recess.

Finally, good children's books leave you wanting more when they are over. They are descriptive enough that your mind can create visuals while reading, but nothing feels too dragged out or rushed toward the end when the mystery is resolved. There aren't any loose ends left hanging because these stories are supposed to teach kids lessons on life in some way. And even if they don't realize it themselves, there must be an underlying message about the power of positivity to take away some wisdom from what they are reading. All in all, writing a good children's book is no easy feat! It takes patience and time spent researching your target audience—children.

Bring pleasure to children during reading.

One of the essential elements of children's books is to please and excite a child. Children's literature experts have repeatedly said that if adult readers are not excited about what they are reading, they will take away excitement from their kids or keep their attention. A study shows that enthusiasm turns into pleasure for both adults and children. The more exciting an adult is when reading to their children, the more likely they will read again. This will be the case even if they are already familiar with the book or reading it many times.

If you want your child to like books, make sure that you enjoy what you read by taking breaks and showing emotion while making appropriate voices and tones for characters in stories. It is essential to consider that children's attention span is not like an adult. Therefore, avoid spending too much time on just one story or passage without letting them interact with what they are listening to. If possible, try some interactive games related to the story before resuming reading again.

These are easier said than done, but it is important to remember that no one starts well at something. Even the best writers write books that are not initially considered masterpieces. Paying attention to details in your writing can help you improve gradually. For example, to be better at dialogue, study other authors' works and see how they have presented conversations between characters. If you want to develop better plots for your stories, look at examples of others' work in different genres and often take on how the conflict was built up or what made readers think about their lives differently after reading a particular story. If you do this, you will improve your chosen path in just a few days because these great writers have taken the time to develop their skills.

You can also improve your writing by doing some background research on the topic you are currently working on. Reading other works in different genres about a similar subject or issue can help familiarize you with various aspects of a particular theme and give you possible ideas for characters, settings, and plots.

To develop writing skills that will please both child readers and possibly adult readers during reading, one should pay attention to details in his/her work and study how great writers have developed their skills over time through practice.

Using a writing service to create a children's book

Whatever the idea's origin, most writers quickly realize that being an author isn't as easy as it looks. From coming up with fresh characters and plots to developing believable dialogue and figuring out how to layout pages so they look good for readers-there is more to writing books than just stringing together sentences.

When writing your book, you first want to realize one simple but important fact: all writing services are unequal. Some writing services will promise high-quality work at rock-bottom prices; others will charge premium rates for only average work. It's important to know that getting published requires quality writing if you're trying to write your book.

You need an experienced writer who has written many children's books and is familiar with what publishers are looking for in terms of style and format for this specific type of writing.

A good writer will also offer guidance on your original idea, so they can help improve it or flesh out parts you haven't considered yet. This means that you get a well-written book with all the right characters, plot twists, and dialogue because the person writing it knows precisely how to make these aspects shine as they should.

The most popular way to find a writing service that can create a children's book for you is to look online. There are tons of them out there, and most will offer competitive prices, flexible rates, and even free samples, so you know exactly what you're getting before you pay anything. Many also promise feedback if you want it, so the more experienced writers on staff can work on your storyline or characters with you until they get it just right.

Because there are so many ways to write a children's book, some services specialize in specific areas rather than offering full coverage. For example, if your story idea features an animal as an essential character, choose a service specializing in animal books. However, if your idea centers around pirates or another "human" character, you'll need to find a more than qualified service in this area.

While getting your book professionally written might sound like an expensive proposition, it can save you money in the long run. Some of today's most popular authors can charge premium prices for their work because they've honed their talent and skill at creating books that sell repeatedly. If you want the same quality in your children's book project, enlisting a writing company's services will help ensure everything turns out great for both author and the reader alike.

Hiring freelance writers on Fiverr

Fiverr is a website that allows individuals to sell their freelance skills or hire others to do tasks they don't have time to do themselves, including writing children's books. Those who sell services on Fiverr are known as freelancers; many offer their services in writing stories for children and editing and proofreading.

Children's book authors with little time but big ideas are turning to Fiverr to create books they can then sell online or use as giveaways to promote their businesses, gather emails of potential customers, or build their brand.

Writers on Fiverr work with the author by creating the story and sending over written samples that the customer later edits until both parties are satisfied.

The process is usually quick, with children's book authors paying freelancers $60 or more to create a book between 20 and 30 pages long. The books are delivered in eBook format and easily published on Amazon to download Kindle devices.

Many sellers offering writing services on Fiverr have been creating stories for years and have even written entire series that they continue to sell online.

Sellers typically offer their stories in picture or comic book formats, catering to potential buyers who may not require a full-length story but need something relevant to their business for promotional purposes. The stories are written in various genres, including mystery fiction, fantasy, science fiction, and poems.

Some sellers offer the opportunity to create books that have already been published but are no longer available online after selling out. This is also an ideal option for children's book authors who may not have the time to sit down and write their own stories but want something new about their creations.

Writing services on Fiverr cost anything from $5 to $60, depending on how lengthy the project is. Prices can sometimes go up if writers use high-end software or specific graphics programs as part of the process.

> My Story: All my illustrators, editors, and musicians for the audiobooks have come from Fiverr. You need to take your time to vet them, but overall, I have been really pleased with the talent. The Nola The Nurse® illustrator has been with me for EIGHT years!

Writers from Upwork

Unknown to many parents and teachers, many of today's hit children's books were written by one person and two or more people working together to write a story for kids. This is because there are simply some things that only another writer could contribute with their expertise in writing for kids with their level of understanding of what appeals to them most.

So, if you need help with great stories or want your child to have access to top-quality books that inspire them to read more, you should consider hiring a freelance writer from places like Upwork. This is a great way to save time and money.

Hiring a freelancer for this type of work makes sense because many writing niches require specific skills, such as writing about subjects related to classical mythology or popular fairy tales. In those cases, it would be next to impossible for an average person to develop relevant ideas and make the story engaging enough for kids, especially if they don't have any children.

The other reason why it makes sense to hire the services of a freelance writer at places like Upwork is that this person will be able to bring their true perspective and expertise. If, for example, you need a children's book about a particular type of animal, a freelancer who has dedicated some years to studying this animal will likely know many things that not even your favorite children's book author would know. For instance, if you wanted a story about an adventurous dog, the best thing would be to hire someone who knows everything there is to learn about dogs. That way, they can provide insights from both an adult's and a child's point of view.

In addition to knowing what kids love most in books, a freelancer will also take care of the illustrations and bring them to life. This was one of the benefits I enjoyed as an author, as it meant that I needed to know how to write for children, but I also had to illustrate my books. As you can see, there are many good reasons why hiring someone who is both a book author and an illustrator is something that any parent should consider doing if they want their child to learn more about great books and grow up into a responsible adult. If you need help coming up with great stories or want your following children's book to be top-quality to inspire children to read more, you should consider hiring a freelance writer from places like Upwork.

Content Writers forums

As a child-book author, you probably know that finding a suitable setting for your work is not always an easy task. Many authors seek professional assistance writing children's books through content writer forums like Facebook content writers' groups while relying on their skills. Due to a lack of time and expertise in fictitious scenarios, most publishers prefer ghostwriters or expert writers over authors whose fiction talents are limited.

While it is widely accepted that after-sales are more important than sales, most publishers believe that the storyline isn't good enough if they cannot relate to it or understand it even by reading just once. So regardless of how good your story is, if the book reader cannot understand and appreciate it in a short period, it isn't worth publishing.

The good news for you here is that many expert children's book authors have done this already, and they know where to get the best from when looking for experienced fiction writers for hire. If you browse online, you will notice many forums where content writer forums offer writing assistance on school research, affidavits, blog posts, thesis works, and other English writings.

Some of the best literary works have been written by experts doing this for a living. Some of these content writers' forums even offer ghostwriting services where they draft the whole story on your behalf before submitting it to publishers for consideration.

As a newbie to publishing children's books, you might not know that many famous publishers have opened their doors online to amateur authors. Still, since most are already busy writing, they can't search for every book publisher. Therefore, they use the services of members of content writer forums, which offer professional writing services on all subjects, including fictitious scenarios like writing children's books.

Freelancers

Making children's stories is not easy. That is why publishers often turn to independent freelancers for children's book authorship. These independent freelancers are often freelance writers who work with businesses or individuals to create unique content.

How do these professional freelance writers work with children's story clients? Well, the explanation is simple: they follow a simple formula. Children's book authorship is not the only thing these freelance writers are hired to do. They are also often contracted to edit other people's stories. The great thing about editing someone else's story is that it gives the writer a clearer feel for what works and doesn't. The writers' method to ensure a good story for children is simple. It's completely different from the process of someone who wants a book written in full. The writer must have an understanding in their mind of what will work and what won't. They should also be in tune with today's market to reach out and grab their audience's attention.

These freelance writers keep up with the times by regularly watching children's shows and reading books. They note what kinds of stories are catching on and which aren't working. This gives them a starting point when they write or edit another person's story. They know what they are working on within today's market, which allows them to create something that will work today.

Professional freelance writers understand what publishers want if you need help editing or writing a children's book. This is why you should turn to their services for help. They will give your project the attention it needs and ensure that your story works for today's market.

Children's Books Covers and Titles

For decades, children's books were only published in black and white. However, today's children's book covers come to life with vivid colors and imagery that can give your ideas for your book. So how do you go about designing the cover of your child?

When designing a kids' book, the experienced designer must understand the age group's primary target audience. If they are young, do not design in bright colors or use complex images just because they may look nice. Young minds have trouble understanding these things until they become more mature. Therefore, the key here is to keep ideas simple and colors easy to see.

If your child's book is for middle-aged kids, you can add a bit of color and flair since they tend to be well acquainted with these things at this point in their lives. The important thing about designing a cover for older children is to make it look appealing to them while displaying the information needed on the cover and in the book. This will ensure that your book gets noticed when looking through the shelves of Barnes & Noble or other local bookstore locations.

Not everything about creating good covers for books has been written yet. This leaves you with questions unanswered, such as: How do you find the right font and size? What is considered a good and bad color scheme, and why? When it comes to knowing these things, some books can help. Some have written these books by the best designers in the business, so it doesn't hurt to read them from time to time as they may give some new ideas on what makes a great cover and some advanced techniques on how to create one.

Remember that children's book covers have a responsibility attached in any event. They have been meant for young minds that need guidance which means being mindful of appropriate images, colors, and layouts that will help promote moral values without scarring them for life. This is because kids' books are supposed to be seen as examples of good and bad so parents can use them to teach their children how they should behave in society.

> Tip: Most illustrators will offer interior AND cover packages. This is often the better deal.

Titles and Subtitles

To be a successful children's book author, you must create a title and subtitle that captures the child's attention. It is about grabbing their attention from the bookstore's kids' section.

I love this book by Robert Sabuda because it ticks off nearly every rule in creating enticing children's books. The artwork has a lot going on, and the colors capture your eye when looking through books at a bookshop. The green lettering stands out against the red background when looking for something interesting to read.

The text boxes provide a new degree of information and difficulty in following up with what is happening in the plot. The main character says he doesn't want to go into the room filled with spiders. The text from another character then says, "Pretty please."

The font plays a considerable role, as it makes the book look more realistic because of the size and movement of each letter. It could be easy to look at all the colors and want to buy this for your child just based on how attractive it seems. The title itself is a statement, and it is a question too.

The main character wants to know what the other one is talking about, and he asks, "What's that?" Then, look at how much more you learn from reading those small words in big lettering. The subtitle explains why he asks that question and gives away a little bit of information as to what his curiosity leads to. Some best-selling children's authors will tell you they spend much time coming up with titles and subtitles because their success depends on it.

Here, the subtitle gives away a little bit of the story without giving too much away. In other words, it is not super descriptive but still manages to tell you what will happen in the story. This is an excellent example; kids and adults love this book because everything looks detailed from beginning to end.

If you want to make a successful children's book, you need to keep your title and subtitles under control because they play a massive role in helping children enjoy the story while also taking some time to think about what might be going on during their read-through.

Cover design rules

The following criteria and guidelines apply, curated from the experience of expert children's books.

- Only an illustration or a figure in an illustration can occupy the entire cover space. If you use another graphic element, it should be smaller than the illustration.
- If possible, only illustrate the main character(s) involved in most of the story's actions.
- There should immediately be something that suggests what genre a book belongs to when looking at its cover.

- The cover should be designed so that the type is either fully visible or placed where it can be hidden by shifting the cover slightly. Avoid setting the type high up where it cannot be read when the book is flat on a shelf.

- It must be clear at first glance what size this book will become after being shrink-wrapped.

- There should be no appearance of special effects used to choose colors for parts of the illustration or elements thereof. This includes making shadows appear as if cast by one element only.

- The illustration must not be difficult to reproduce in black and white.

- Create a picture that looks different when seen from another angle than which one is normally presented with when the book is placed right halfway on a shelf, for example. If this includes showing something through a window created by an open door, do not forget to close the door again before putting it back down flat on its cover.

- The entire spine width should contain type or images, including all run-in text [type running along the edge between the spine and front cover, basically], even if the book has been divided into chapters. Avoid splitting the type into two separate lines when designing covers with more than one chapter title.

- The font type should be the same size and weight as that found in the body of the text.

- The picture and title must clarify what age group this book belongs to at first glance, even when seen from half a meter away while the book has been shrink-wrapped.

- The illustration should appear three-dimensional if possible. Avoid creating pictures that might result in difficulty distinguishing whether the illustration itself or its colors are shiny or decorated with glitter.

- The laminated cover should be matte dull rather than glossy.

- If it is a picture book with several images, one illustration will take up more than 50%

of the total space occupied by images. If possible, the size of the illustrations should also vary.

- The characters illustrated in children's books must not look too much like anyone else's. Use only types and colors that appear in nature and avoid all decorative typefaces.

- Make certain that any text can easily be read when seeing through frosted windows. Avoid placing pictures hiding behind them where those looking at the cover cannot see what is written there without removing the book from its shrink-wrap or holding it at an odd angle to do so. It is good if the outline of a window frame can be seen when holding the book at an angle, but not if one must tilt one's head to read anything behind it.

- The horizon should never fall inside any element other than the sky. It is also important that no text shall be included below this line. If people are illustrated, they should always be standing on ground level, and their feet must preferably not be covered by shadows so that they appear closer to the reader than the text.

- Avoid covering too many illustrations with type, making it difficult to distinguish what is part of which image. Make sure that the text is placed to balance the overall picture.
- It is all right to illustrate elements, but they must be more symbolic than realistic, so it is possible to tell what these stand for without reading the book first.
- Avoid illustrating impractical things that might later prove difficult when designing title pages where one must show more than one page at a time. Create images that allow text in all four corners and can easily be cut in two without distorting anything.

CHAPTER 4

Book Bleed and Formatting

What is a book bleed?

Bleed, also known as a safe zone, is the margin outside the trim size that allows for additional printing or cutting of a book without losing any vital information. What makes it into that extra space should be anything that will appear missing if it's cropped away. It can consist of vital story elements such as a character's hand or a bit of cover art. The first thing to consider is the medium in which the final product should be printed. The two main options namely:

- Offset printing
- Digital printing.

Offset Printing: In this process, ink is transferred from a plate attached to a rotating cylinder onto a rubber-blanketed cylinder which transfers ink to paper moving underneath it. This means that bleeds cannot accurately be communicated by saving files with no trim box or bleed margins included. There must instead be a half-inch gap around all edges of the page so that ink can go from edge to edge without being cut off by the trimming process. This is because offset printers have a minimum of 2-3mm thickness to their plates, so any print from it will also need to be at least 0.5-1 mm thick to avoid losing information.

Digital Printing: Printer resolution can be set as low as 75 pixels per inch, which means that the edges of images and text will become jagged - generally unacceptable for a professional result. The same concerns about bleeds apply here - if setting your document up for printing on a digital press, ensure the file contains bleed margins and no trim box or scale information has been saved.

What should you know about the book dimensions?

In children's books, picture books usually range from 7.5" x 8.5" to 9" x 10", and board book sizes vary depending on how thick the book is, ranging from 2" wide by 4" long up to 6" square.

The best bleed size for children's book

Board Books: 3.75" by 4.875" or 1/2". The spine may be 1/4", but the same amount should be kept on each side - so essentially, 3/8" would remain after cutting. This is because board books are generally cut to shape; rather than trimmed down, which means that only straight lines are required. Picture Books: 5" x 7.5". These are printed at a ratio of 4:3, meaning they appear squashed if not printed with an image area of at least 22 "-24% larger than the trim size (so 26-28% larger for this particular case). This leaves room for 1/8" bleed all around the edge of the page. Chapter Books: 5" x 8.5". These are printed at a ratio of 1:1, meaning they appear as squares if not printed with an image area slightly larger than the trim size (so 16-18% larger for this case). This allows for 1/8" bleed all around. Hardcover picture books and chapter books: 9" x 10". They should contain no less than 24% extra space, so 28% larger will be fine in this case and allow for a 3/8" bleed all around the edge of the page. Children's eBook - Make sure your document contains 3mm bleeds and has no scale information saved into it.

eBook formatting and its essence

Each year, children's books continue to grow in popularity. Many children's book authors wish to sell their books on different electronic devices, such as computers, tablets, or smartphones. Getting an eBook formatted correctly for these devices isn't always easy. First, an author must decide to format their book themselves or hire a professional. Many formatting guidelines must be followed for the eBook to look good and be readable on all devices. Authors must take certain factors into account before using an online service. Ensure that they receive a sample of this service before paying for the formatting. Some companies will only send proof to an author after paying substantial money, which is unfair.

If a company does not provide samples on its website, there might be some reason.

In some ways, hiring a professional eBook formatter is the best option if you want your book to look perfect on all devices. However, this can be very expensive; some authors do not have enough money to invest in this service. Some people decide to format their books because it is cheaper, and they think it's easy enough to do with just a bit of research online. Many programs can help an author format an eBook for a specific device. However, these programs can be complicated and usually need to be purchased at a high cost. The main drawback of using one of these formats is that they are sometimes incompatible with certain devices, or the file types produced might not work correctly.

When formatting an eBook, specific guidelines must be followed to look good on any device. One of the biggest mistakes that authors make when they self-format is putting pictures where they should not go or inserting them upside down. The program should also allow the text to reformat itself if users change their screen size. If this happens, this will make the book more enjoyable to read and easier for the eyes of users who are continuously scrolling up and down while reading each page.

You must research the best method to get your children's book formatted correctly. Hiring a professional can be very expensive but provides high-quality results. Self-formatting can take longer, but it is cheaper than an outside service. Even if you decide to format the book yourself, certain guidelines still need to be followed to look good on all devices. If you format your book correctly the first time, it will take far less time to do so after you've finished writing it.

People of all ages on different devices are constantly buying books. The main reason why children's books are continually growing in popularity is that they entertain while teaching something new. Formatting can be challenging for an author if they do not know the formal requirements that need to be followed. If an author follows the appropriate guidelines when formatting their book, there is a strong chance that it will look good on any device and allow readers to enjoy reading it easily.

CHAPTER 5

Before Book Publishing and Marketing

After proofreading and editing your book, you should review it for simplicity. Read it aloud several times, then read it to a 7th grader, asking them to point out anything they did not understand. If there are too many problems with the wording or sentence structure, rework the sentences, making them easier to follow.

Ensure you know which age group the book will appeal to and whom you might recommend this book to at school libraries or other institutions. Once you have written your manuscript, write a press release about your books and send copies of this information to potential reviewers in education journals or newspapers. If appropriate, you should also do some library visits, which means contacting local schools and libraries in advance to arrange to visit dates where you can describe your new children's books and read some extracts.

List the information below on web pages to promote your book.

List each item as a link within the body copy, so you have one piece of writing, but it appears you have three separate items.

List image captions using sentence case, only capitalize the first word, with no ending punctuation at the end of each caption.

List image titles in all caps, with ending punctuation after each title.

Images are linked to their source and not directly to an image file. This way, if future changes are made to this page, your images will remain consistent with the writing.

First, review your book for anything that may cause questions or confusion for parents or other children's books fans.

Next, write a press release about your book and send this information to potential reviewers in education journals or newspapers. If you are so inclined, do some library visits as well. This means contacting local schools and libraries ahead of time to arrange dates when you can describe your new children's books and read the extracts selections.

Finally, list all the following information on one set of web pages to promote your new book. You can create these pages/posts using any website-building platform.

Book Marketing

The publishing industry is an important part of modern life that authors find themselves in. The core of the publishing business are writers, editors who work closely with them, publishers who give their input about what sells best and how to promote books effectively, booksellers who sell the publications, librarians who help readers discover new titles they will enjoy reading, book clubs which spread the word among customers about books to read. Marketing professionals significantly impact the quality of children's books sold well in stores.

The marketing plan for each book starts when the author gets an offer from a publisher based on her proposal or completed manuscript. This is when they sit with professional marketers to discuss strategies for promoting her work and planning its release to the public. Everything from book jacket design and typeface selection to pre-publication reviews and book club promotions is considered, and authors may even give input on the overall marketing strategy.

An effective marketer for children's books:

- understands what kids like and want to read about;
- creates a marketing plan that will tap into kids' interests;
- targets her message at readers of specific ages or maybe younger or older readers;
- The number of units necessary to sell for it to be successful is called the break-even point;

- Tries to get an idea if this book will be best promoted in bookstores, through media, or both.

As part of her marketing plan, the author will want to decide whether this is a long-term project with multiple titles or if it's one-time only. If she has more books planned for this series or these characters, she'll want to build opportunities for readers to learn about new titles and make them aware of where they can purchase copies. A children's book publicist may be brought on board at this stage to help develop effective press releases and pitches for media such as newspapers and magazines.

Copyright and Trademarks

A copyright is a legal protection for the creator of original work, whether writing, art, music, or architecture. For writers who create characters and stories, their characters and stories are automatically copyrighted by creating them. This does not protect against someone else creating similar characters and/or plots, but it DOES protect your written works from infringement, such as unauthorized copying and distributing.

A trademark is a word, phrase, symbol, design, sound mark, or group of letters used to identify certain goods and services as those produced by a specific individual or company. For example, when we see "Coca-Cola" on a soda bottle, we buy the Coca-Cola company's product. Trademark protection does not protect against someone else using similar marks, but it DOES protect trade names and brand names such as book titles and character names.

Why should you care about copyright and trademarks?

Trademarks protect your marketing efforts. Without trademark law, somebody could slap their name or brand on your book cover, and you would have no recourse without pursuing legal action to stop them. Copyright protects your product from infringement, meaning nobody can steal your art and call it their own.

> My story: I hired a Trademark and Copyright attorney. It has been the best investment yet! Trademark attorneys can work on your behalf nationwide because trademarks are federally registered. This means they can live anywhere and help you. Her name is Attorney Kimra Major-Morris with the Major-Morris Law Firm out of Florida. Again, best investment for Brand protection, EVER.

Amazon book market research and tips

Your primary goal as an author should be to sell books. But now and then, it doesn't hurt to remind ourselves of our goals as self-publishers because they don't always include selling lots of books or making tons of money for some of us. It can be helpful if you remember why you started writing in the first place: the love of stories. Your book might not save lives or win awards, but nobody can take away how important it is to **you**, even if only one person reads it.

As authors of children's books, there are additional hurdles to successfully marketing your books. Let's look at how we can overcome the challenges in front of us and find success as self-publishers.

Tips for market research

1) Start with Amazon bestseller lists in your category. Note how of both specific age groups and genders. Look for similarly themed books and check out their Amazon product descriptions to see what formats they're selling in (hardcover, paperback, eBook), the links provided, and what other people say about them in the reviews.

2) Don't tell, show: When it comes to marketing children's books online, there is a simple rule of thumb:

    A) Never talk TO your audience because you will sound like a salesperson but

    B) Always talk ABOUT your audience so they feel heard while giving helpful information that will ultimately benefit THEM.

- Imagine you've looked up a children's book, and the reviewer mentioned what they liked and didn't like about it. What would they be saying?

- Are they complaining that certain scenes or topics were inappropriate or too scary? Are any of those scenes in your book? Would this be something that readers want to know before buying your book?

- Marketing is not just advertising: Book marketing is all about reader engagement. This means getting people excited about reading your story, so they'll share it with others. Here are some tips for engaging your audience:

A) Use keywords and SEO (Search Engine Optimization): Which words do you think people will type into the Amazon search bar when looking for books like yours?

B) Regularly update your social media page: People want to know what you're up to and value relevant and interesting posts.

C) Give out free books as part of a promotion: Ensure the eBooks you distribute through Smash words or Draft2Digital have universal book links (UBLs). When readers click on those UBL, they will be taken to whichever retailer sells your eBook; in this case, it would be Amazon.

D) Create Book Trailers: A book trailer uses images and video clips to tell the story in a motion graphic style like movie trailers. These can be powerful promotional tools for both print and eBook formats. Conduct interviews with experts and reviewers in your field: The more educational value your book provides, the better.

Other marketing channels

Apart from Amazon and offline marketing, below there are effective marketing platforms used by expert children's books authors:

Website

Children's book authors and illustrators must take advantage of all available marketing opportunities. The adage "If you build it, they will come" does not work for marketing children's books.

An often-overlooked method of product promotion is to use a personal website to market and promote your children's books. Nowadays, everyone has a personal website: friends, family, neighbors, and even babies' birth announcements, including web page information. Why not add a link to your author or illustrator's website from your site? This should be no problem since it promotes you as an author or illustrator.

What can children's book authors and illustrators whose publishers do not provide such services add to their websites? A children's book author or illustrator might consider adding the following to a personal site, depending on his/her abilities:

- They have a biography of themselves and a list of all published works with links to each book's product pages.

- A high-resolution version of their most recent cover art can be used anywhere. This is particularly helpful for display at schools, public libraries, and other venues that don't carry eBooks. The PNG format is preferred since it preserves transparency.

- Additional artwork for teachers to use in classroom projects that are not available under any licensing.

- Information about upcoming releases, readings, and events. Information can be automatically updated if managed through one central source.

Spend some time looking at other author and illustrator websites for ideas on what to include on your site. It should include images of the author or illustrator and professionally taken photos showing the book covers they have illustrated or authored (not selfies taken with a phone). The professional photos would help readers envision how you would look in person if they had the chance to meet you at one of your readings, signings, and school visits. The cover images will show why your books are popular and why people might want to purchase the books you have illustrated or authored.

However, an author's website should include more than contact information and a list of published works. Some authors go beyond themselves and add information about the people they write for.

Marketing through Google Play

Google Play is a digital store that sells music, movies, books, and apps. It's attached to Google's Android operating system, which runs on many smartphones and tablets currently on the market. People buy many things through Google Play: more than 25 billion apps have been downloaded since it opened in October 2008. In addition to buying, people can get free versions of books through 'sample' downloads. A sample download lets you read part of a book for free before deciding whether to buy it.

When you write a children's book, promoting your book by giving out samples is an excellent way to create awareness amongst potential readers. Getting children to read your book is the first step in recommending it to their parents, who are the ultimate decision-makers.

How to promote a children's book on Google Play

To begin with, you need to have a Google Play account. When your account is set up, log into it using the same Google ID for your Amazon Kindle Direct Publishing (KDP) account. KDP is where authors upload their digital versions of books once they've finished writing them and made any necessary edits. Books are available on Amazon within 48 hours of uploading them. However, if you want to sell your book through Google Play as well as Amazon, follow the steps listed below:

- Create an account with Google Play—it's free.
- Add your book to Google Play. You can do this even if it's already on Amazon, if you use the same Amazon ID for both accounts.
- Look up the proper category for your book and ensure it is correctly categorized; otherwise, people will not find it when they search the store.

Decide how much you want to charge for your digital book. Free books are available, but people usually won't bother looking at them because they expect a product on Google Play to have a price tag.

Sample downloads boost sales of children's books. People who download a sample of your book on Google Play are more likely to purchase it than those who read an excerpt on Amazon. Paid samples cost between 99 cents and $2.98, which you'll have to pay out of your royalties. However, with a little creativity and planning, you may be able to turn what would ordinarily be a loss into a profit. For example, if your book targets the 8-12 age group and each chapter ends with a cliffhanger that leaves children begging for more by buying the rest immediately, you could charge for each chapter.

Use tags to ensure your book is easy to find on Google Play. Tags are keywords people put in when they're looking for something specific.

Ingram Spark

The most critical aspect of successfully marketing a book is to have your book in as many outlets as possible. Ingram Spark covers most major worldwide markets for self-published authors. It's a service that allows you to upload a digital file of your manuscript and, if accepted, will create multiple copies of "proofs" for each title you publish through the service.

It also creates traditional print books on demand (POD). Allow at least ten business days before you receive printed copies of your book. You should set up an account several months before your anticipated publication date.

Since Ingram Spark will be the record printer, they distribute traditional print and digital versions. You can either place your listing with Bowker or allow Ingram Spark to do so on your behalf. Either way, it costs $150 per title and can take anywhere from 8-12 weeks after upload to show up in their system.

Once your book is listed with Ingram Spark creates a listing for you, information about the title will be sent out to various industry directories, including Baker & Taylor's Books in Print database. These databases are often accessed by libraries and other institutions who have purchased or wish to purchase your book.

The Ingram Spark website will allow you to locate where your book is being sold in the world.

> My Story: I frequently use the app: Ripl. It's a paid app and I am not a spokesperson for them, but it has been helpful for us and it is fairly cheap.

CHAPTER 6

Book Publishing

The world of children's book publishing is constantly changing, with old methods falling out of favor and new ideas taking their place. More authors choose to self-publish, but there are still takeaways from traditional publishing that are just as relevant now as they have been in the past. Below is a breakdown of the publishing options available to children's book authors.

Traditional Publishing

Traditionally published books are those in which a publisher provides the author a contract, and in exchange, the publisher prints, publish and distributes your book to bookshops and other retailers. The publisher, in essence, purchases the right to publish your book and pays you royalties on the book's sales.

Simple steps to publish children's books traditionally.

- Perform extensive research to determine what publishers are the best fit for your manuscript/concept; find out whom they accept submissions from generally their website, snail mail address, or agent; and where you can purchase examples of their books which you should study to help you decide if this publisher is right for your project.

- Write a query letter describing your book idea. This letter should be very concise and include the following information:

    1. The title of your proposed book

    2. A brief description of your proposed book

    3. Your qualifications for writing this book, including previous writing experience and degrees in literature or education.

- If you have an agent, you should include their information if they pitch to a specific publisher on your behalf; otherwise, say 'undisclosed.'
- Send the query letter and proposal only when the publisher requests that exact format (general guidelines state that it is usually no more than 1 page long at most but check with their submissions department first). Do not send the same query to multiple publishers at once; it will be seen as unprofessional and may result in rejection from all publishers who receive it because your cover might accidentally get detached from one copy and stuck to another.
- Wait for a response. A standard time frame is four months, and if you do not receive one after that period has elapsed, send them a polite note inquiring about the status of your submission. If you still do not hear back from them in another month, assume it is rejected and move on.

It's preferable to get feedback than none at all because it shows the publisher likes your concept but perhaps does not want to invest in it at this particular point in time or their list is full; however, if they were just flat-out rejecting it without any comments whatsoever, then find someone who will take the time to give you specific reasons why the publisher rejected your project and review any pointed out.

Self-publishing and its promise of freedom

One of the main reasons authors choose to publish their works is recognition. Before self-publishing, it was much more difficult for an author to get noticed in an industry where publishing companies pick up only a select few. There is no middleman and more potential ways to stand out from the crowd with self-publishing.

Self-published books have several advantages over traditionally published ones: they can be published quickly and remain available indefinitely, whereas traditional publishers will only print a limited number of copies simultaneously. They also demand less money upfront or none, making them considerably cheaper than traditionally published titles. Self-published authors do not have to wait on anyone else's schedule but their own, meaning they can release books as frequently or infrequently as they want. However, one of the downsides is that self-published eBooks make significantly less money than traditionally published ones.

Joint publishing

Joint publishing (or co-publishing) is a business model for publishing books in which an individual or organization publishes its content with another publisher to reach an audience. Joint publishing deals that make sense are mutually beneficial and result in greater exposure, recognition, profit, and sometimes stock.

In joint publishing, two authors may split their book's profits while collaborating on its subsequent releases if they continue to create books after the initial release date. If one or both decides not to continue working further on the project, they can "pass" it on to a third party, who will receive all rights and royalties. The book goes forward to publication as long as it remains complete.

Joint publishing is a parent company that publishes books jointly by two or more authors. The most common joint effort is between two authors of the same age, both of whom have a background in writing books for teenagers, for example, two high school students who write about love and romance but want their work available to an even wider audience - their parents and teachers.

A joint publisher is like an imprint within a traditional publishing house that focuses on specific genres and releases limited quantities of books under its imprint. For instance, if a traditional publisher is known for its romance novels and wants to increase the number of books it puts out through its branch company, it can create a joint publishing deal with two romance novelists and turn their book into a novel published through their imprint. The imprint then handles rights and royalties while the two authors negotiate future agreements.

In joint publishing, you receive up to 50% of profits on the books you are credited for. Profit is generated when a book sells more than five hundred copies at full retail price. If a discount store or online retailer sells your book for less than full price, you only receive half of the profit from your book once it reaches **$250** in sales. It can result in a loss-making product if discount stores, or online retailers buy only a few copies.

To be considered eligible for a joint publication, you must have been published by the same company previously and have at least one book in print that is selling. If you meet these requirements, you will agree with the publisher as an author and work with them to publish your next book under the same imprint.

Vanity Publishing

While vanity publishing is a relatively common practice in the writing world, many who choose to publish their work via this route remain unaware of the terms and details that come with it. Vanity publishing allows authors to write and publish a book without waiting for traditional publishers to accept their work or read multiple revisions if they submit it. A typical vanity publisher will publish your book, including formatting, editing, and promotion.

In other words, vanity publishers can provide you with your finished product once completed and give you exclusive rights over how it's distributed. Of course, they do this for a fee, but generally, it's a lot less expensive than the amount you would pay an agent and a traditional publisher.

CHAPTER 7

Book Publishing Companies

Publishers are responsible for producing the written works of authors and technical matters. The publishing industry is divided into many categories, such as the following:

- Trade Book Publishers.
- Book Packagers and Book Developers.
- "Bargain" Book Publishers
- Book Development Companies
- Textbook Publishers and Academic Publishers.
- Professional Publishers.
- Self-Publishing Services.
- Hybrid Publisher

Trade Book Publisher

A trade book publisher publishes and distributes books. They are responsible for selling the books they publish to retailers. A trade book publisher has marketing, sales publications, and distribution expertise. A trade book publisher helps expert children's books publish their books by offering resources that make it easier for experts to get their ideas published in the first place.

Trade book publishers do not sell their books in bookstores. Instead, they sell their books through distributors who take the trade book's orders from retailers. For a trade book publisher to profit from selling each copy of a given trade book, they need retailers ready, willing, and able to purchase all the copies of that title at any given time.

Book Packagers and Book Developers.

Book Packagers and Book Developers for children's books authors.

Several book packagers and book developers specialize in helping children's book authors do the publishing legwork. There are many benefits to using these specialists, but you need to know exactly what they can do (and what they can't) before deciding. This article is intended to help you.

Book Packagers

Book packagers companies take care of the printing and binding of your book to concentrate on writing. You (the author) must fill out their forms, provide them with any writing samples that the company requests, and decide what you want to include in your books, such as which chapters should be on the front and which should be in the back or appendix, and provide them with information about how you want your book to look. Most package companies require that all of this be done before sending out a proof copy, so make sure this is what you want.

Most book packagers can also help you with promotions, such as arranging for speaking engagements or sending out press releases, and they can do some of the marketing and site-design work so that you don't have to do it yourself.

Book Development Companies

Book development companies are involved in every aspect of your book, from writing, editing, designing, and formatting. They help you turn your manuscript into a book that people will want to buy by helping you ensure that it is well-written, entertaining, grammatically correct, and easy for readers to navigate. Book development companies can advise on the best way to market your book, from deciding on a title to creating eye-catching and informative websites.

"Bargain" Book Publishers

Publishing a children's book as an author can be a great experience. It can also be costly, especially for those not experts in the field. This is where "Bargain" Book Publishers come to play. They offer valuable services that allow non-experts to publish their work and make it available for distribution and sale worldwide. From editing and formatting services to printing and marketing, "Bargain" Book Publishers offer everything necessary for successful authors — without the prevalent cost of publishing fees or royalties typically associated with other channels. The most important part of this equation is that the publishing costs are minimum. "Bargain" Book Publishers do not charge authors for their services, allowing them to pay only for those who will move their books. They also do not require authors to pay licensing fees, allowing them full creative control over their work.

For an author who does not want to engage in traditional publishing because of its high cost, "Bargain" Book Publishers are a great alternative. Instead of relying on publishing houses or other established avenues to publish and distribute your book, you can use "Bargain" Book Publishers as your publisher.

Textbook Publishers and Academic Publishers

Academic publishers sponsor scholarships and research written on thesis or research books. It is important to remember that some publications want children's books for review or as extras in their print editions. These places differ from traditional publishing houses, like traditional publishers who publish many bestsellers yearly.

The publishing industry has grown substantially over the years, and so have its options for finding new material. The industry produces millions of titles annually, but navigating without an editor, agent, or publisher guiding you through these waters can be difficult.

There are hundreds of places where you can find your book reviewed, but to ensure you're reaching the correct audience and getting the most out of your investment, you'll need to be very clear on what each of these publications' reviews. The first thing is to know what academic publishers review.

Professional Publishers

Once you have that information, you must decide which publication is best for your project. Most independent children's books authors find it difficult to make ends meet, so a popular outlet maybe cost prohibitive. They compete with other authors so that pressure can compromise publishing standards.

Children of all ages love children's books. Most children's books are available in paperback and sometimes in hardcover. The most common way to purchase a child's book is online or through your local library and bookstore. You can also buy these books from an independent bookstore if you live near one. There are many publishers for children's books, so choosing which publishing company to use can be difficult. Children's books are books that are published for children.

The children's book publishing industry is a multi-billion-dollar business. It is the third-largest publishing industry in the U.S. and the fastest-growing book industry. Children's literature is a broad genre and includes various works such as picture books, middle-grade books, young adult novels, and children's magazines. It is not a very competitive industry because most published books are sold through established publishing houses. This is why most people who try to publish children's books independently don't succeed.

Choosing a publisher can be difficult because there are many different children's book publishers to choose from. It would help if you looked for a publisher with a proven track record publishing a similar book to the one you are trying to get to market. You should also research and find out if the publishing company is reputable. You can use the internet to find out about companies by reading reviews and testimonials on their websites, but you should be careful about believing everything you read online.

Self-Publishing Services

Self-publishing is the process of writing or illustrating your book and, in most cases, distributing it directly to customers without having a publisher involved. Self-publishing has become more popular in recent years because of the lengthier processes associated with finding a publisher, especially as beginning authors often do not have enough money to pay for printing. In addition, many people have trouble working with outside organizations after experiencing rejection from publishing houses. There are many reasons why an author would want to self-publish.

Some of these include:

If you want to self-publish because of the long process of finding a publisher, or if you do not have the money to pay for printing, it makes sense to use services such as those offered by Self-Publishing Services.

Self-Publishing Services provide the tools you need to write, edit, and publish your book. These services can be used for both nonfiction and fiction children's books and young adults. Many authors self-publish their books because they enjoy writing them more than working with a publisher.

Hybrid Publisher

Many children's authors are turning to hybrid publishing services to help them get their books out faster and at a lower price. Here's how you can use these services for your book-writing projects.

It is always better to have a second opinion regarding books, especially for young children. Even if it is just some feedback about the pacing or characters that might affect the entire story, feedback from a professional can improve the quality of your work and make it more marketable.

The most popular methods in publishing today are online self-publishing and print-on-demand. Still, several other options, including hybrid publishing, may provide better results than traditional publication.

Hybrid publishing involves taking the same material that a traditional publisher would use and converting it into a format that can be published through print on demand. This format can then be sold in bookstores or through the hard copy version. The cost to publishers and authors is much less than traditional publishing and eBook printing while maintaining quality control and distribution. It is an excellent solution for authors who want to get their work out there but cannot spend months editing and proofreading due to time constraints.

> My Story: I decided to develop my own publishing company. The name is A DrNurse Publishing House. I found this to be easier to manage and allow me to keep the lion's share of profits from each book sale. It's set up just like a traditional business. It is an LLC; has its own EIN; and the name is trademarked. Of course you also need a bank account because it is a legal business and a place where you want to legitimately receive royalty checks. Also, all my logos are developed from Fiverr talent.

CHAPTER 8

ISBN and Different Prefixes

The International Standard Book Number (ISBN) is a thirteen-character code that uniquely identifies books and tells booksellers where to send them to be ordered. ISBN-registered publishing agencies assign International Standard Book Numbers (ISBN). The International Standard Book Number Association (ISBN) sets the rules for composing the correct ISBN code, and you can find them on their official website.

The rules may seem rather complex, but they're not too complicated to remember. Remember that International Standard Book Number (ISBN) should be composed based on three main aspects: the author's surname, first name or pen name, and the book's title. Let's look at some of these rules in more detail.

The most important aspect of an International Standard Book Number (ISBN) is its prefix. This number is reserved for publications that are:

- Fiction and narrative nonfiction
- printed on pages bound together
- publications with standard size and form

Its publication address is in the United States of America.

The prefix 979- can be used for books, brochures, journals, or pamphlets that are:

- musical scores with or without words for instruments, vocals, or any combination of instruments and voices. This includes any accompanying printed material. Not just music books but also sheet music. If you write music books that include original compositions, this rule applies to them;
- illuminated manuscripts, manuscripts written in calligraphy, and manuscripts that have been bound like greetings cards and postcards;

- a publication with an ISBN assigned during the last 12 months because the publishing company has new owners or is reincarnated.

To put the prefix 978- or 979- in front of a book's title, you must purchase it from one of the companies authorized by the International Standard Book Number (ISBN) Association. Otherwise, your ISBN won't be valid. The only exception is a self-published book whose author has their own ISBN prefix.

What children's book authors should know about ISBN

The ISBN for your publication should be applied as soon as you submit your manuscript and before you start editing, rewriting, or printing it. You can apply for your ISBN conveniently through Bowker, an international indexing firm that forms the backbone of this process.

The sooner you apply for your ISBN, the earlier you receive it. For children's books, you can get an ISBN within days. If you prefer to wait until your manuscript is completed, it will take a little longer to get your ISBN. ISBNs are assigned to new books or reprints in a paper-covered hard or softcover format that matches the previous edition's ISBN, no matter what country they were published in.

However, applying for your ISBN is essential as soon as you submit your manuscript and before you start editing, rewriting, or printing it.

> My Story: I purchased a pack of 100 ISBN's and have been able to save $$$. It's also nice to have all of your books with closely numbered ISBN's if they are all in a series.

Conclusion

I hope this short book helps you on your journey to becoming a children's book author. It was meant to be short, sweet, and effective. You literally can write a children's book AND publish it in 24 hours! Let's Goooooooooooo!!!!

I am wishing you so much success and always will be cheering you on. Welcome to the world of children's book writing! I can't wait to purchase and review your work.

Schar

More books by Dr. Scharmaine Lawson

Fiction

- Nola The Nurse®, She's On The Go Series Vol 1 (available in Spanish and French)
- Nola The Nurse® & Friends Explore The Holi Fest, She's On The Go Series Vol 2
- Nola The Nurse® Activity Book for Preschool Vol 1
- Nola The Nurse® Activity Book for Kindergarten Vol 2
- Nola The Nurse® Math Worksheets for Kindergarten Vol 3

- Nola The Nurse® English/Sight Worksheets for Kindergarten Vol 4
- Nola The Nurse® Math/English Worksheets for Preschoolers Vol 5
- Nola The Nurse® Math Worksheets for First Graders Vol 6
- Nola The Nurse® STEM Activity Book for 5–8-year-olds Vol 7
- Nola The Nurse® & Friends Explore The Holi Fest She's On The Go Series Vol 2 Coloring Book
- Nola The Nurse® Remembers Hurricane Katrina Special Edition
- Nola The Nurse® Remembers Hurricane Katrina Special Edition Coloring Book
- Nola The Nurse®: Let's Talk About Germs, The Germy series, Vol. 1
- Nola The Nurse®: How To Stop Those Yucky Germs, The Germy series, Vol 2
- Nola The Nurse® & her Super Friends Learn About Mardi Gras Safety, Holiday series, Vol 1 (Fall 21' release)

- Nola The Nurse® Cursive Handwriting Workbook For Kids
- Nola The Nurse® Science Word & Puzzle Search For Kids
- Nola The Nurse® Mandala Coloring Book for kids
- Nola The Nurse® Coloring Book for Kids
- Black Dot

Non-Fiction

- Housecalls 101: The only book you will ever need to begin your medical practice, Part I
- Housecalls 101: A Clinician's Guide To In-Home Health Care, Telemedicine Services, and Long-Distance Treatment For a Post-Pandemic World, Part II
- Housecalls 101 Policy & Procedure Manual
- Culture Stories: Racism, Bias, and Prejudice in Nursing (soon to be released)
- Pandemic Parenting

- www.NolaTheNurse.com
- www.DrLawsonNP.com

🎙 Podcast

Nite Nite Nurse Podcast

- https://open.spotify.com/show/3nGnfpXTUfVUx2mQTrsWrG?si=1881e7a2728545fe
- DrLawson@DrLawsonNP.com

www.ingramcontent.com/pod-product-compliance
Lightning Source LLC
Chambersburg PA
CBHW011408070526
44586CB00021B/2580